W9-AFF-723

AMISH COOKBOOK

TABLE OF CONTENTS

AMISH LIFESTYLE

AMISH FAMILY LIFE

Although extinct in their European homeland, the Amish have flourished in the United States and Canada. Three factors have contributed to their success: A high birthrate, cultural isolation and a willingness to strike compromises with the modern world. The Amish people cherish their children and treat them with deep respect and love. A high birthrate promotes Amish growth. An Amish family typically has six to nine children. The rejection of birth control and the use of modern medicines have helped to boost the Amish population.

Amish parochial schools effectively socialize children through the eighth grade and immerse youth in traditional lore and thought. The taboo on high school and college effectively insulates Amish youth from modern thought and values. Until they start to school at the age of six, most Amish children speak little English. The primary language spoken in the home is "Dutch," a Pennsylvania German dialect. The use of Pennsylvania Dutch, a child's native tongue, shapes a unique world view and binds members together, drawing a sharp line between insiders and outsiders.

Horse transportation limits travel and, hence, interaction with the outside world. Taboos on political and social involvement in community organizations also restrict social contacts. The rejection of radio, television, and other mass media insulates the Amish family from secular values. The Amish family however is not a calcified relic of a bygone era. Part of their success lies in their willingness to compromise with modern life. The Amish don't own or drive cars but they frequently ride in cars and buses. Tractors are used around Amish barns, but not in the fields. Community telephones appear at the end of farm lanes, but not in homes. Electricity from twelve volt batteries are widely used, but 110 volt from public utilities is forbidden.

Horses pull modern farm machinery through Amish fields. Modern gas appliances, rather than electric ones are found in Amish kitchens. Gas lamps illuminate modern bathrooms in Amish homes. The Amish strike a delicate balance between the forces of tradition and the sway of progress.

When older family members retire from farming, they often move into a "Grandpa House" adjacent to the main farm house. Retired family members continue to work, doing useful chores around the farm while maintaining a strong sense of independence.

A network of Amish practice and tradition encircles members from cradle to grave. There are occasional trips to town for shopping or to a non-Amish doctor, dentist, or accountant, but for the most part, members live in an Amish orbit. With their work, play, worship, and family, the Amish have created an alternative society, an Amish world that offers emotional security, meaning, identity, and belonging.

SPRING SAMPLER

CHICKEN POT PIE

2	cups chicken, cut in chunks	2 ½	Tbsp. pimento pieces
1	cup chicken gravy	2	cups mashed potatoes
1	can peas & carrots	1	9-inch pie crust

Heat cut up pieces of leftover chicken in a pot with enough chicken gravy to cover it. Add cooked or canned peas and carrots and pieces of pimento. Line the bottom of a deep square or round dish with mashed potatoes. Cover the potatoes with the chicken mixture. Slice pie crust into long strips, about 1" wide. Create a lattice work by placing the strips over the pot pie one way and then crosswise. Put a strip around the edge of the pie and bake at 375 degrees for 20 minutes or until nicely browned.

FRESH ASPARAGUS

2	lbs. fresh asparagus	⅛	tsp. paprika
1 ½	tsp. salt	3	Tbsp. butter
2	cups plus 1 Tbsp. water	2	Tbsp. flour
2	egg yolks	⅓	cup blanched almonds
1	Tbsp. lemon juice		

Cook asparagus with 1 tsp. salt in 1 cup boiling water until tender. Drain asparagus; keep warm. In a double boiler, combine egg yolks, 1 Tbsp. cold water, lemon juice, remainder of salt and paprika; beat well. Melt butter in a saucepan, blend in flour and stir in 1 cup boiling water. Cook, stirring constantly over low heat until thickened. Pour into egg mixture, stir and cook until smooth. Place asparagus on a serving platter. Spoon sauce over asparagus and sprinkle with almonds.

CREAM CHEESE HALO WITH STRAWBERRIES

1	envelope unflavored gelatin	½	tsp. almond extract
¼	cup cold water	1 ¼	cups milk
1	pkg. (8oz.) cream cheese, softened	1	cup heavy cream, whipped
½	cup sugar	1	pt. strawberries
•	Dash of salt		

Soften gelatin in cold water. Dissolve over hot water in a double boiler. Combine cream cheese, sugar, salt, and extract; blend until smooth. Gradually add milk and gelatin mixture to the cream cheese mixture. Chill until partially set. Fold in whipped cream. Pour into a 1 qt. ring mold, and chill until firm. Garnish with strawberries around the mold and in the center.

"The Lord is my Shepherd I shall not want."

-Psalm 23:1

SUMMER BOUNTY

CHICKEN CROQUETTES

2	Tbsp. butter	2	cups saltine
2	Tbsp. flour		cracker crumbs
1	cup milk	4	cups bread
2	cups ground,		crumbs
	cooked chicken	1	tsp. salt
4	eggs, beaten	⅛	tsp. pepper

Melt butter in a small saucepan over medium heat. Add flour, stirring constantly, gradually adding milk until a smooth paste is formed. Stir in chicken. Remove from heat, and let cool. Shape chicken mixture into croquettes. Dip each croquette in cracker crumbs, beaten eggs, and bread crumbs. Place in a shallow casserole dish. Bake at 400 degrees for 25 minutes.

STUFFED TOMATOES

4	large tomatoes	2	tsp. oregano
¼	cup chopped celery	1	tsp. grated Parmesan cheese
½	cup chopped onion	1	tsp. bread crumbs
½	green pepper, chopped	2	Tbsp. butter
1	pkg. bacon, cooked & crumbled	•	Salt & pepper

Cut out the core of each tomato. Combine celery, onions, peppers, bacon, oregano, and salt and pepper to taste. Stuff each tomato evenly. Combine Parmesan cheese and bread crumbs; sprinkle over each tomato. Top each with a pat of butter and bake at 350 degrees for 45 minutes.

EGGPLANT BAKE

2	medium eggplants (to yield 1 ½ cups cooked & mashed)	3	cups bread crumbs
		3	eggs
1	cup milk	3	Tbsp. butter, melted
⅔	cup grated, medium, sharp Cheddar cheese	1	tsp. salt
		•	Dash of pepper

Peel eggplant. Chop into 1" squares. Boil in salted water for 12 minutes. Drain and mash. Combine mashed eggplant, bread crumbs and remaining ingredients in a bowl. Spoon mixture into a large shallow casserole dish. Bake at 350 degrees for 1 hour.

BLACKBERRY CAKE

3	eggs	2	cups blackberries,
1 ½	cups sugar		crushed
1 ½	cups shortening	3	cups flour
2	tsp. cinnamon	2	tsp. baking powder
1	tsp. cloves	1	tsp. baking soda

Combine eggs, sugar, shortening, cinnamon and cloves in a large mixing bowl; beat until well blended. Add blackberries and remaining ingredients. Pour into a greased 13" X 9" X 2" pan. Bake at 350 degrees for 35 minutes or until done.

"If you have not often felt - that joy of doing a kindly act - you have neglected much and mostly yourself."

AMISH FARMING

The most enduring image of Amish life, after the horse drawn Amish buggy and distinctive dress, is the neat, well-manicured Amish farms found in 23 states and Ontario, Canada.

The Amish have become known as some of the world's most productive farmers. Although Amish farm homes, barns, and out building are typically neat and well maintained, the farms are usually not more than 80 acres. The average Amish farm in

Lancaster County, Pennsylvania is 50 acres. Amish farms are family farms, with livestock, field crops, vegetable gardens, fruit trees, and flower gardens.

The Amish farm has changed a great deal over the last century. Hydraulic water pumps have largely replaced hand pumps and windmills. In the barn, cows are milked with vacuum machines and large bulk tanks store refrigerated milk. Old fashioned hand

plows have been discarded for automatic riding plows pulled by horses. Tractors are common on Amish farms, however, they are seldom used for field work. They are used for power around the barns. They blow silage to the top of large silos, power feed grinders and hydraulic systems, or pump liquid manure. The Amish distinction between barn use and field use was, in essence, a way to protect the horse which evolved as the prime symbol of Amish identity. The unwritten rules of the church control the speed of change in Amish life. Church leaders evaluate innovations and those considered harmless eventually slip into practice. If, however, they think a new practice will harm the community they will forbid it. This was the fate of personal computers in 1986. They required electricity and leaders feared the computer might eventually lead to television and they asked members to "put it away."

Not all Amish are able to farm today because of the high cost of farmland and limited acreage. Many newlyweds are turning to carpentry, carriage building, manufacturing horse drawn farm implements, and hand crafts.

Regardless of the task, the Amishman's objective is to complete his work "as unto the Lord."

FALL'S FINEST

BREAD PUDDING

¾	cup white bread cubes	⅓	cup sugar
4	cups milk, scalded	4	eggs, lightly beaten
1	Tbsp. butter	1	tsp. vanilla
¼	tsp. salt	½	cup raisins

Soak bread cubes in hot milk for 5 minutes. Stir in butter, salt and sugar. Pour over eggs and add vanilla and raisins. Stir well and pour into a greased 2 qt. baking dish. Set dish in a large shallow pan of hot water, and bake at 350 degrees for about 50 minutes or until firm. Best when served warm.

SWEET POTATO ROLLS

1	cup mashed sweet potatoes	3	Tbsp. sugar
3	Tbsp. butter, melted	5	cups sifted flour
1	pkg. active dry yeast	1	cup powdered sugar
1¼	cups warm water	3	Tbsp. orange juice
1	egg	1	Tbsp. grated orange rind
1	tsp. salt		

Combine sweet potatoes and butter. Dissolve yeast in ½ cup warm water; add to sweet potato mixture, stirring well. Add egg, salt and sugar; blend well. Add flour alternately with remaining warm water, mixing well. Turn out onto a floured board; knead well. Place in a greased bowl; cover. Let rise for 2 hours in a warm place until double in bulk. Roll out on a floured board and form into desired shapes; brush with melted butter. Place on a greased cookie sheet or in muffin pans, cover and let rise again until double in bulk. Bake at 425 degrees for 15 minutes. Combine powdered sugar, orange juice, orange rind, and a dash of salt; spread over hot rolls.

FUNERAL PIE

1	cup seedless raisins	2	Tbsp. grated lemon rind
1½	cups sugar	•	Juice of 1 lemon
¼	cup flour	•	Pinch of salt
1	egg, beaten	2	9-inch pie crusts

Soak raisins in water for 3 hours; drain. Mix sugar, flour and egg. Add grated lemon rind, lemon juice, salt and raisins. Cook in a double boiler for 15 minutes, stir occasionally. Let mixture cool; pour into a pie crust and cover pie with a lattice top. Bake at 400 degrees for about 40 minutes or until lightly browned.

BARBECUE MEATBALLS

3	lbs. ground beef	1	onion, chopped
2	cups quick oats	2	tsp. chili powder
2	cups milk	2	tsp. salt
2	eggs, beaten	½	tsp. pepper

Barbecue Sauce:

1	cup ketchup	2	Tbsp. liquid smoke
1	cup water	½	tsp. garlic powder
1 ½	cups brown sugar		

Combine meatball ingredients and stir well. Form into golf ball size pieces and place in a baking pan. Combine barbecue sauce ingredients, stirring well. Pour over meatballs, coating well. Bake at 350 degrees for 1 hour, baste often.

"Life is like a grindstone; whether it grinds you down or polishes you up; depends on what you are made of."

APPLE DUMPLINGS

6	medium apples	½	tsp. salt
2	cups flour	⅔	cup shortening
2 ½	tsp. baking powder	½	cup milk

Sauce:

2	cups brown sugar	¼	tsp. nutmeg
2	cups water	¼	cup butter
¼	tsp. cinnamon		

Peel and core apples. Sift together flour, baking powder, and salt. Cut in shortening until crumbs are the size of small peas. Sprinkle milk over mixture, and press crumbs together lightly, working dough only enough to hold it together. Roll dough as for pastry, and cut into 6 squares. Place an apple on each square and fold pastry to surround apple. Place in a casserole dish. Combine brown sugar, water, cinnamon, and nutmeg in a saucepan. Cook for 5 minutes then remove from heat. Add butter and stir. Pour sauce over dumplings. Bake at 375 degrees for 35 to 40 minutes. Brush pastry with sauce twice during baking.

SAUERKRAUT-CARROT SALAD

1	can (16 oz.) sauerkraut	½	cup shredded carrots
¼	cup sugar	½	cup green pepper
½	cup chopped celery	¼	cup chopped onion

Drain sauerkraut; combine sauerkraut and sugar in a bowl. Chill for 30 minutes. Add remaining ingredients and refrigerate for 12 hours before serving.

Note: If homemade sauerkraut is desired, follow these directions. Shred 5 lbs. of cabbage into narrow strips, add 3 Tbsp. salt and toss well. Pack tightly into clean quart jars. Fill jars with boiling water. Close lids loosely. Put jars in a dish pan; juices will overflow as sauerkraut starts to ferment. Close lids tightly after 10 days. Store.

DUTCH BOY POTATOES

1	small onion	•	Salt & pepper to taste
1	Tbsp. butter	•	Milk
4	medium potatoes, cooked & sliced	1	pkg. (8 oz.) shredded Cheddar cheese
¼	cup flour		

Saute onion in butter and add sliced, cooked potatoes. Sprinkle potatoes with flour and add salt and pepper to taste. Brown potatoes on both sides and add enough milk to thicken; simmer on low heat for 20 to 30 minutes or until potatoes are tender. Before serving, top with shredded cheese and simmer until cheese is melted.

"Wisdom is the principal thing; therefore get wisdom...She will place on your head an ornament of grace."

-Proverbs 4:7 & 9

AMISH FOOD

The Amish people are well known for their cooking, a culinary tradition that they shared with other German-speaking immigrants who came to Pennsylvania in colonial times. In those early years of German immigration, their language, traditions, folk art, and style of cooking became known as Pennsylvania Deutsch, (or German), mispronounced Dutch. It is a style of cooking that emphasizes hearty food that will sustain people who do hard physical work. Amish dishes retain many German influences today.

Amish meals are wholesome and satisfying. Food is plentiful, but not extravagant in preparation. There is certainly enough, but the quantity is never excessive. While grains, wheat, barley, rye, and corn are typical crops on Amish farms, a portion of the land is always reserved for fruit trees, and a kitchen vegetable garden. An important part of the Amish tradition is self-sufficiency.

The kitchen is the heart of the Amish home, which is also often the warmest room! This is the room where the whole family meets for each meal, and of course, for conversation and companionship. From the time an Amish girl can walk, she is in the kitchen helping her mother. Amish children help with chores around the house and farm as soon as they are able to do so.

Canning is also a major part of Amish cooking. Nothing is left to go to waste. All of the produce from the orchard and garden is used in season, and the rest is put up to be enjoyed all winter long. If you lived in an Amish community you wouldn't think of going to the supermarket to buy corned beef. You would make it yourself...probably 20 pounds or more. Sausage making would be the same. You and your neighbors might

cure and smoke 100 pounds of ham at a time or dry or can 100 pounds of beef, all to be used throughout the year.

When the Amish came to this country, they brought with them seeds, considerable farming skills, and their favorite recipes. But like other immigrates who came to call the United States home, the Amish had to adapt their recipes to what was available in the new land. So while their recipes speak German, they do so with an American accent. That is as it should be, because however different they may appear, the Amish people are a part of our national history and a part of our culinary history, as well.

FIRESIDE FAVORITES

POTATO BUNS

5	eggs	2	cups lukewarm
¾	cup shortening		water
1	cup sugar	2	cups mashed
2	Tbsp. salt		potatoes
3	Tbsp. yeast	7 ½	cups bread flour

Beat eggs; add shortening, sugar and salt. Beat again. Mash potatoes and add to egg mixture. Beat well. Dissolve yeast in lukewarm water. Add flour, mix well. Place in a greased bowl. Cover and let rise in a warm place for 2 hours or until double in bulk. Punch down, cover and let rise again. Roll out 1″ thick and cut with a round cutter. Place on a greased cookie sheet, cover and let rise again until double in size. Bake at 350 degrees for 20 to 30 minutes or until lightly browned.

*"She watches over the
affairs of her household,
and does not eat the
bread of the idleness."*

-Proverbs 31:27

ALMOST TURKEY

2	lbs. hamburger	4	cups milk
2	cans cream of chicken soup	1	loaf of bread, broken
1	can cream of celery soup	•	Salt & pepper to taste

Mix the above ingredients and form into a loaf. Bake at 350 degrees for 45 minutes.

CHEESY CREAMED BRUSSELS SPROUTS

3	lbs. brussels sprouts	½	cup shredded Emmentaler or
2	Tbsp. butter		Muenster cheese
2	Tbsp. flour	4	strips bacon, cooked & crumbled
½	pt. whipping cream	½	cup seasoned bread crumbs
¼	tsp. fresh nutmeg	•	Butter
•	Salt & white pepper to taste		

Remove the outer leaves of the brussels sprouts, cut off the stems, and soak in salted water about 20 minutes. Drain. Add to boiling water; simmer for 5 minutes. Drain. Melt butter in a pan over low heat, and slowly stir in flour. Gradually add the cream and cook slowly until the mixture begins to thicken. Grate in nutmeg, and stir well. Add the shredded cheese and stir mixture until the cheese melts and add the bacon. Season with salt and white pepper to taste. Place brussels sprouts in a greased casserole dish. Pour the sauce over the top. Sprinkle the seasoned bread crumbs over the top, and dot with butter. Bake at 350 degrees for 30 minutes or until hot and bubbly and nicely golden brown.

CHICKEN & BARLEY SOUP

1	whole stewing hen	2	tomatoes, chopped fine
1	qt. water	3	celery stalks, chopped very fine
¼	cup barley grains		
2	carrots, diced	•	Fresh parsley, chopped
½	cup mushrooms, sliced	•	Salt & pepper
1	onion, chopped		

Combine all the ingredients, except salt and pepper, in a stew pot, bring to a boil, and simmer for 1 hour. Remove chicken, drain and reserve stock. Cool, debone and cut chicken into small pieces and put back in the stew pot with the rest of the juice. Reheat, salt and pepper to taste, and serve.

DOUBLE RICH AMISH CHEESECAKE

3	eggs	•	Pinch of salt
1	cup sugar	1	tsp. lemon juice
1 ½	lbs. cream cheese (not lowfat), softened	1	prepared graham cracker or chocolate cookie pie crust
½	pt. double cream or whipping cream		
2	Tbsp. flour		

Notice as you read this recipe, there is a lot of beating needed to make this a success. Beat the eggs and sugar in a large bowl, until the mixture is extremely thick and creamy. In a separate bowl combine cream cheese, flour, salt, lemon juice, and cream and beat thoroughly. Combine contents of the two bowls and beat again. Pour the mixture into the pie crust and bake at 350 degrees for 1 hour 15 minutes. The cake will rise as a souffle would. Turn off the heat and let the cake rest and settle with the oven door partially open for 30 minutes. This is a truly basic, good, rich, cheese cake!

BEETROOT BORSCHT

1	lb. brisket	2	potatoes
1	qt. water	3	cups shredded cabbage
1	qt. beef stock	4	medium carrots
1	tsp. salt	¼	cup butter
4	thick slices bacon	6	sprigs parsley
1	large onion, chopped	3	peppercorns
3	stalks celery, chopped	•	Fresh dill
2	cloves garlic, chopped	•	Freshly ground black pepper
1	bell pepper	•	Sour cream
4	medium beets		
2	cups fresh or canned plum tomatoes		

Simmer brisket in the beef stock and water. Add salt and cook for 1 hour. Remove and reserve brisket. Fry the bacon in a skillet and set bacon aside. Saute the chopped onions, celery, and garlic in the bacon drippings. Drain. Cut up the bacon, and add to the stock. Peel and cut up the bell pepper, beets, tomatoes, and potatoes into chunks; add to the stew pot, plus the shredded cabbage. Dice the carrots, saute them in the butter, and add them to the stock. Add seasonings and bring to a boil. Reduce heat; simmer for 45 minutes. Cut the brisket into chunks and add them to the soup. This makes a wonderfully tasty, rich soup. Serve in large bowls and top with a dollop of sour cream.

"A little of the oil of Christ like love will save a lot of friction."

DEEP-DISH PEACH COBBLER

1	cup self-rising flour	1	Tbsp. lemon juice
1	cup sugar	1	tsp. cinnamon
1	cup milk	1	qt. sliced peaches
½	cup butter, melted		

Stir together flour, sugar, milk, butter, lemon juice and cinnamon. Pour into a buttered 9" X 13" X 2" casserole dish. Add peaches; do not stir. Bake at 350 degrees for about 30 minutes or until golden brown.

CREAM OF CABBAGE COUNTRY SOUP

2	Tbsp. butter	1	cup julienne carrots
2	Tbsp. flour	1	cup slivered onions
2	cups milk	1	tsp. dill
2	cups chicken broth	2	bay leaves
2	cups shredded cabbage	•	Salt & pepper
2	cups cubed potatoes		

Melt butter in a sauce pan; add flour stirring constantly. Gradually add the milk and the chicken stock. Add cabbage, potatoes, carrots, and onions. Season with finely chopped dill, the bay leaves, salt and pepper to taste. Simmer until all the ingredients are tender. Add more milk or water for desired thickness. Remove bay leaves before serving. This is a particularly nice soup for a light luncheon.

AMISH RELIGION

The cultural roots of the Amish community are religious. Many of their practices are expressing a simple piety - a desire to be faithful to God. Religious meanings permeate every aspect of their culture, yet they forgo church buildings, choirs, altars, organs, stained glass windows, Sunday school classes, and professional pastors. They do not evangelize or support missionaries and avoid most of the trappings of religious institutions.

body of Christ "pure and spotless" from the contaminating stains of the world. The Amish stress the importance of obedience, humility, and simplicity as fruits of a faithful Christian life.

Amish youths usually join the church in their early twenties, but must do so before they are married. "Rules of Order" set by the bishop govern the local church district. The rules which govern the Amish community cover almost every aspect of their lives.

They include the style of buggies, the type of buggy wheels, the length of hair for men, (the women do not cut their hair), the width of hat brims, and the length of beards, etc.

Although the Amish disdain many of the outward symbols of modern religious life, their faith permeates the entire fabric of their community life. It is a

The Amish affirm the basic tenets of Christian faith. Baptismal candidates are instructed in the Anabaptist Confession of faith written in 1632. The Amish believe that the Bible is Gods word, and that Jesus is God's Son, who died for their sins, and that the church is the body of Christ, fulfilling God's purpose on earth. The Amish emphasize the importance of keeping the

practical piety, expressed by wearing plain clothing, raising a barn for a neighbor, coming to the aid of disaster victims, or baking a pie for a sick friend. It is a religious faith anchored in the strength of traditional values, rather than in an emotional "religious" experience or ostentatious sacred ritual.

SUNDAY TRADITION

SWEET DILL PICKLES

•	Cucumbers	1	cup vinegar
1	slice onion	2	cups water
1	head dill	½	cup sugar
1	tsp. dill	2	Tbsp. salt

Fill a 2 qt. bowl with cucumbers, add next 3 ingredients. Stir together vinegar and remaining ingredients until all is dissolved. Fill bowl with brine; pour into hot jars. Place jars on a rack, in canner, in hot water. Cover with 1" hot water. Cover canner loosely and bring to a boil for 5 minutes. Remove jars from canner onto a rack or towel; let sit undisturbed for 12 to 24 hours. Yield: 2 quarts.

CRACKER PIE

3	egg whites	24	round butter crackers, crushed
1	cup sugar		
1	tsp. baking powder	1	tsp. vanilla
1	cup pecans	•	Whipped cream

Beat egg whites until stiff. Gradually add sugar while stirring. Fold in the remaining ingredients. Pour into a greased pie plate. Bake at 350 degrees for 25 minutes. Top with whipped cream.

SANDWICH SPREAD

6	cups cucumbers	3	cups sugar
4	cups onions	6	Tbsp. butter
3	red sweet peppers	3	Tbsp. flour
3	green peppers	3	Tbsp. mustard
6	Tbsp. salt	1	tsp. celery seed
4	cups vinegar	1	cup cream
3	large eggs, beaten		

Grind cucumbers, onions, sweet and green peppers using a coarse blade. Add salt, stir and let stand 2 hours. Add 2 cups vinegar, and bring to a boil; drain and press dry. Combine remaining vinegar, eggs, sugar, butter, flour, mustard and celery seed to the vegetable mixture; cook for 5 minutes. Add cream and bring to a boil, then pack into hot jars, and seal. Place on a rack in a canner filled with simmering water; cover jars with 2" hot water. Cover canner loosely, and bring to a boil. Simmer gently for 20 minutes. Cool on a towel for 12 hours.

"Give us this day our daily bread."

-Matthew 6:11

PICNIC PANTRY

SAUSAGE MACARONI CASSEROLE

1	pkg. (8 oz.) elbow macaroni	3	Tbsp. flour
1	lb. bulk pork sausage	½	tsp. salt
½	cup onion, chopped	2	cups milk
½	cup green pepper, chopped	2	cups Cheddar cheese, shredded

Cook macaroni in 3 qts. of salted water for 7 to 8 minutes. Drain well, and set aside. Brown sausage in a saucepan, remove and reserve ⅓ of the sausage. Saute onions and green pepper with remaining sausage in the pan. Stir in flour and salt; slowly add milk; stirring constantly, and cook over medium heat until thickened. Stir in 1 ½ cups cheese. Combine macaroni and sauce. Spoon into a greased 2 qt. casserole dish, and top with remaining cheese and reserved sausage. Bake at 400 degrees for 25 minutes or until browned and bubbly.

SNICKER DOODLES

1	cup shortening	1	tsp. baking soda
1 ½	cups sugar	¼	tsp. salt
2	eggs	1	Tbsp. sugar
2 ¾	cups flour	1	Tbsp. cinnamon
2	tsp. cream of tartar		

Cream together shortening, sugar and eggs. Sift together flour, cream of tartar, baking soda, and salt. Add the dry ingredients to the creamed mixture and stir well. Roll into small balls. Combine sugar and cinnamon; roll each ball in the sugar mixture. Bake at 375 degrees for 8 to 10 minutes.

THANKSGIVING PUMPKIN BREAD

3	cups sugar	2	tsp. baking soda
1	cup oil	1 ½	cups pumpkin,
4	eggs, lightly beaten		cooked & mashed
1	tsp. cinnamon	⅔	cup water
1	tsp. nutmeg	1	cup walnuts,
1 ½	tsp. salt		chopped
3	cups flour		

Combine sugar and oil; mix well. Stir in eggs. Blend in cinnamon and remaining ingredients. Pour into a greased 8 or 9-inch loaf pan. Bake at 350 degrees for 1 hour.

CREAMY COLD POTATO SALAD

10	medium potatoes, cooked	•	Salt & pepper to taste
6	hard boiled eggs	½	cup mayonnaise
6	green onions, chopped	1	Tbsp. vinegar
3	ribs celery, chopped fine	1	Tbsp. sugar
1	bell pepper, diced small	2	Tbsp. spicy dark mustard
•	Small jar pimento bits	½	pint heavy cream
½	cup sweet pickle relish		

Cook potatoes until tender. Let cool and dice potatoes into medium sized chunks. Peel eggs, chop whites, and save yolks. Mash the yolks with the mayonnaise to give the salad a nice yellow color. Add all the chopped vegetables, pimento bits and sweet relish and toss lightly, but very thoroughly, so the salad won't become one big lump. Add vinegar, sugar, mustard and cream to mayonnaise and egg mixture. Drop over the salad in large spoonfuls and toss lightly again. Put the salad in a shallow bowl or enameled pan so it will chill thoroughly. If you use a deep bowl, the salad may not get chilled in the center and will spoil. Place it in the refrigerator overnight.

"Thy word is a lamp to my feet and a light to my path."

-Psalms 119:105

AMISH EDUCATION

The Amish are not opposed to education, but they fear that public education and higher education will pull their children away from their traditions and the Amish way.

Until 1950, the Amish attended one room public elementary schools. These public schools were compatible with Amish values and in the rural schools, Amish youth in some areas, were in the majority. As public schools consolidated, state laws tightened and required youths to attend school to the age of 15, which usually meant going to the ninth grade. Amish protest galvanized against such laws, and between 1950 and 1955, dozens of Amish parents were arrested and imprisoned each fall. The clash between Amish parents and school authorities led to the rise of Amish parochial schools and a home base vocational education program.

Amish leaders decided to build their own one room schoolhouses and after several years of discussions with public officials worked out a compromise that complied with the compulsory school law, forcing Amish youth to attend the ninth grade at public high schools.

The compromise, called the Amish Vocational Program, permits Amish 14-year-old's to attend a weekly vocational school in an Amish home after completing the eighth grade. For three hours a week an Amish teacher instructs a dozen or so youths in vocational skills such as business math, reading, and writing.

In 1972, the U.S. Supreme Court conferred its legal blessing on this arrangement for the Amish school system. Today, Amish children attend their own local one room elementary schools with an average of around 30 pupils. The schools are often within walking distance of the child's home.

To preserve their traditional culture and prevent the loss of their children on the alter of progress, the Amish were forced to snub public and higher education. It was a comprise that allowed the Amish to preserve traditional ways and steer their youth toward adult involvement in the Amish community.

BREAKFAST BEST

SPATULA EGG SCRAMBLE

1	cup diced bacon	12	eggs, beaten
¼	cup chopped green onion	1	can (3 oz.) mushrooms,
3	Tbsp. butter		chopped

Cheese Sauce:

2	Tbsp. butter, melted	2	cups milk
2	Tbsp. flour	1	cup shredded Cheddar
½	tsp. salt		cheese
⅛	tsp. pepper		

Topping:

¼	cup butter, melted	2 ½	cups soft bread crumbs
⅛	tsp. paprika		

In a large skillet, saute bacon and onions in butter until tender. Add eggs and scramble just until set. Remove from heat; set aside. Prepare cheese sauce, by blending butter into flour, salt and pepper; add milk gradually. Cook, stirring constantly until bubbly. Stir in cheese until melted. Fold cooked eggs and mushrooms into cheese sauce. Spoon into a 7" x 12" baking dish. Combine the topping ingredients, and sprinkle over the egg mixture. Cover and refrigerate overnight. Remove from the refrigerator 30 minutes before baking. Bake uncovered at 350 degrees for 30 minutes.

PHILADELPHIA STICKY BUNS

¾	cup milk	1 ½	cups dark brown
⅓	cup sugar		sugar, packed
1	tsp. salt	½	cup currants, soaked
¼	cup butter, melted		until plump, drain
2	pkgs. active dry yeast	½	cup chopped pecans
⅓	cup luke warm water	1	Tbsp. cinnamon
1	egg, slightly beaten	¼	cup butter
4	cups flour	1	cup dark corn syrup

Scald milk; stir in sugar, salt, and butter. Cool to lukewarm. Dissolve yeast in warm water. Stir in milk mixture, egg, and 2 cups flour. Beat until smooth; stir in enough of the remaining flour to make a soft dough. Turn onto a floured board; knead for about 8 minutes or until smooth and elastic. Place in a greased bowl; turn to grease the top. Cover and let rise in a warm place for about 1 hour or until double in bulk. Mix ½ cup brown sugar with currants, pecans, and cinnamon. Set aside. Mix remaining brown sugar, butter, and corn syrup; bring to a boil. Pour into 2 square pans; cool. Punch dough down; divide in half. Roll each half to a 9" X 14" rectangle; spread with butter. Sprinkle each rectangle with half the pecan mixture. Roll up as for jelly roll and seal edges. Cut into 1" slices and place, cut side down, on the syrup mixture. Cover; let rise again for about 45 minutes or until double in bulk. Bake at 350 degrees for about 25 minutes or until light brown. Invert on a plate and cool.

"Doubt sees the obstacle.
Faith sees the way.
Doubt sees the darkest night.
Faith sees the day."

MID-DAY SNACKS

SOFT PRETZELS

1	pkg. dry yeast	¼	tsp. salt
1 ½	cups warm water	1	egg, beaten
4	cups flour	•	Coarse salt
1 ½	tsp. sugar		

In a large bowl, dissolve yeast in water. Add flour, sugar and salt; mix well. Knead on a floured surface until smooth and satiny. Shape and twist into pretzel shape. Brush with egg and sprinkle with coarse salt. Bake at 350 degrees for about 10 to 15 mintues or until golden brown.

HOMEMADE ROOT BEER

1	tsp. active dry yeast	1	qt. hot water
½	cup warm water	4	tsp. root beer extract
2	cups sugar		

Dissolve yeast in warm water. Dissolve sugar in 1 qt. hot water. Combine dissolved yeast, sugar liquid and root beer extract in a gallon jar. Fill jar with warm water and stir until all ingredients are well combined. Cover jar; set in the warm sun for 4 hours. The root beer will be ready to drink the next day. Chill before serving.

BUTTERSCOTCH TAPIOCA

6	cups boiling water	1	cup milk
1	tsp. salt	½	cup white sugar
1 ½	cups small pearl tapioca	1	cup of butter
2	cups brown sugar	1	tsp. vanilla
2	eggs, beaten		

In a saucepan, mix water, salt, and tapioca; cook for 15 minutes, stirring constantly. Add brown sugar and continue cooking until done. Add eggs, milk, and white sugar. Return back to the heat and cook until it bubbles. Brown butter and vanilla. Cool and top with whipped cream, bananas, and diced candy bar.

CHERRY PIE

2	cups red sweet cherries	1	Tbsp. clear jel
1	cup sugar	1	tsp. almond extract
¾	cup water	2	9-inch pie crusts

Mix cherries, sugar, and water; bring to a boil. Mix clear jel with enough water to make a paste. Add this to the boiling cherry mixture, stir constantly until thickened. Remove from stove and stir in the almond extract. Pour into the pie shell and top with crust. (may slice crust into strips to form a lattice crust top) Bake at 425 degrees for 30-40 minutes or until done.

MOTHER'S TOMATO SOUP

6	onions	1	cup butter
2	red peppers	¼	cup salt
10	qts. fresh tomatoes	1	cup flour
1	cup sugar		

Cut vegetables into small pieces. Cook vegetables in 1" of water until soft. Put through a food press and place in a saucepan. Bring to a boil. Add sugar and the remaining ingredients. Cook until butter and sugar are dissolved. Place soup in hot jars and seal. Place jars, on a rack in a canner, in hot water; cover jars with 2" hot water. Cover canner loosely. Bring water just to a boil. Simmer for 30 minutes. Yield: 8 quarts.

"While traveling along the road of life, enjoy the going and stop thinking so fiercely about getting there!"

AMISH WEDDINGS & HOME LIFE

Courtship for many Amish young people is one of the favorite seasons of their lives. Love is instilled as a lifetime commitment to a mate. Amish weddings are not arranged, but courtship takes place within the framework of clear shared expectations. One of the main social activities for Amish young people is a "Singing." Several hundred young people may attend. The tempo of the music sung may be faster than the slow unison chant of Sunday church service.

Amish young people traditionally do not have an extended engagement period before marriage. Public announcement of the intention to marry is normally made several weeks before the wedding by the deacon or the bishop. Most weddings take place after the harvest is finished, in November and December.

The wedding day may begin as early as 5 A.M. and continue until late at night. Relatives, friends, and members of the church district are invited in person or by postcard. Guests may arrive before dawn and are greeted by a hand shake by the bride and groom. The bride has probably made her own dress–white is not used. Dark colors are preferred; dark blue or purple are used in Lancaster county. The groom and his attendants wear the traditional white shirt, black suit, and black felt hat.

The wedding service parallels a regular church service. The wedding could last three hours or longer, with scripture readings, two sermons, and much singing. Marriage is for life; divorce is not an option! The remainder of the day is spent in feasting, singing, and visiting. The wedding season is the high point of Amish social life. In many communities, the newly married couple will not take up housekeeping until spring. They will spend long weekends together visiting friends and families. It is at this time that wedding gifts are given. The groom's family will generally help with the financial responsibilities of getting the new couple established.

Wedding time is followed by seasons of bearing children and additional financial responsibilities. Child rearing suddenly becomes the most important task for the young couple. No other expression of love or one's Amish faith surpasses the care and nurturing of one's children.

WEDDING FEAST

OLD-FASHIONED STUFFING

1	cup chopped celery	1	can cream of chicken soup
½	cup chopped onion		or 1 ¼ cups chicken gravy
½	tsp. poultry seasoning	8	cups dry bread cubes
¼	cup butter		

Saute celery, onions, and poultry seasoning in butter until vegetables are tender. Mix in soup and add bread cubes. Mix stuffing until all ingredients are moist. Yield: 4 cups.

ROAST DUCK WITH APPLE & PRUNE DRESSING

1	duck	1	can chicken stock
•	Salt & pepper	1	cup orange juice
1	pkg. cornbread dressing	1	tsp. orange zest
1	large apple, cut in chunks	1	Tbsp. brown sugar
1	small pkg. pitted prunes		

Rinse duck with cold water; pat dry. Sprinkle with salt and pepper, inside and out. Prepare cornbread dressing according to package directions. Mix apple and prunes with cornbread dressing. Fill the cavity with the dressing mixture. Roast in a 400 degree oven for 15 minutes. Then reduce heat to 350 degrees and roast until browned. Remove from the pan, pour off the excess fat, and deglaze the pan with the can of chicken stock. Cook, stirring constantly until sauce begins to thicken. Add orange juice and orange zest. Stir in brown sugar, and return the duck back to the pan. Bake until the skin is crusty and the sauce is well cooked, basting the duck often.

"Rejoice with them that rejoice, and weep with them that weep."

SHOOFLY PIE

Pie crust:

⅔	cup flour	½	tsp. ginger
1	tsp. cinnamon	⅓	cup butter
½	tsp. nutmeg		

Add the spices into the flour and stir well. Cut the butter into the flour with a pastry cutter or with two crossed knives. Work this together until well mixed, but toss it lightly. Do not make one heavy lump. Place on a lightly floured board and roll out to the size of the pie plate. Fit the pie pastry into the pie plate, carefully pushing it well into the bottom and edges. Bake it just lightly enough to set it.

Pie filling:

½	cup brown sugar	2	eggs, beaten
1	tsp. soda	2	cups flour
1	cup hot water	¾	cup brown sugar
1	cup molasses	¼	cup butter

Combine brown sugar and soda in hot water. Add molasses, and eggs; stirring well to blend. Pour into the partially baked pie shell. In a separate bowl, mix flour, brown sugar, and butter until crumbly. Sprinkle evenly over pie. Bake at 325 degrees for 10 minutes; reduce oven temperature to 300 degrees and continue baking for 35 minutes.

"Prayer should be the key of the day and the lock at night."

SCALLOPED SWEET POTATOES

4	cups sweet potatoes	1	tsp. flour
1	cup brown sugar	½	cup cream

Boil sweet potatoes in salted water until tender. Dice sweet potatoes and put in a greased casserole dish. Mix together brown sugar, flour, and cream. Pour over sweet potatoes and bake at 350 degrees for 20 to 30 minutes.

WIENER SCHNITZEL

8	veal cutlets, trimmed	•	Seasoned bread crumbs in a large shallow bowl
•	Salt & pepper to taste		
3	eggs	•	Lard or vegetable oil

Place ovensafe platter in a 250 degree oven; keep warm. Rinse cutlets with cold water and pat dry with paper towels. Flatten with a kitchen mallet and season with salt and pepper. Beat eggs with a small amount of water. Melt the lard in a large skillet over medium-high heat. Dip cutlets in egg mixture and then dip in the bread crumbs until well covered. Fry them in the lard. Reduce the heat as they brown. Place cutlets on platter in the oven. Garnish with lemon wedges, cherry tomatoes, and a border of parsley or endive. The name means that these are cutlets cooked in the manner of Vienna.

MARINATED COLESLAW

1	head cabbage	1	bell pepper, chopped
½	cup cane or rice vinegar	2	Tbsp. mustard
½	cup sugar	1	cup mayonnaise
•	Salt & pepper to taste	•	Milk or half & half cream

Slice or chop a head of cabbage finely. Add the vinegar, sugar, salt and pepper to taste and chopped bell pepper. Mix thoroughly and place in the refrigerator overnight. Mix mustard with the mayonnaise. Add a little milk (or half and half cream) to desired consistency and mix thoroughly. Possible additions: Chopped peanuts or drained crushed pineapple.

SPUD PORK CHOPS

2	medium potatoes, sliced	4-6	pork chops
•	Salt & pepper	•	Milk
1	cup chopped onion	1	cup bread crumbs
1	small green pepper, chopped	2	Tbsp. butter

In a greased baking dish place a layer of sliced potatoes and season with salt and pepper to taste. Cover potatoes with onion and green pepper. Sprinkle pork chops on both sides with your favorite seasonings and place on top of onions and peppers. Add enough milk to moisten the ingredients. Sprinkle bread crumbs on top, dot with butter and bake at 350 degrees for about 1 hour and 15 minutes or until done.

AMISH DRESS & BUGGY

There is no uniform style of dress among the Amish, although the basic elements are generally the same. Bonnets, hats, and dress colors vary a great deal from district to district, but the principles are the same. The Amish believe that a Christian will look different from the world in his or her appearance.

Unmarried teenage girls normally wear a white covering during the week and a black covering on Sundays. On her wedding day the bride wears a black cap for the last time. Amish women wear black caps over their white coverings for special occasions and during the winter.

Customarily everyday work clothes are made by mother or girls old enough to make their own dresses from yard goods. But Sunday dress suits, for both men and boys, are made by a seamstress who buys large rolls of suiting from wholesale fabric suppliers.

Men and boys dress suits are finished out with hooks and eyes on coats and vests. Buttons are not used on coats because the European soldiers who persecuted the Anabaptists in the 16th century used large buttons on their uniforms. The pacifist Amish avoid any resemblance to the military. In a fashion-conscious America, the Amish dress may appear quaint. However, for the Amish it emphasizes separation, simplicity, and modesty.

The most obvious symbol of the Amish is their horse-drawn buggy. There are nearly 100 different types of horse drawn vehicles among the Amish. The average buggy costs two thousand to three thousand dollars, depending on the style and the community. Horse auctions are common because few Amish raise their own horses.

Weather can become a major factor in buggy transportation. Some groups forbid the closed-in buggy; some drive buggies with open fronts; some forbid any top. Riding in these open-buggies require heavy clothing, blankets, an umbrella, and a pioneer spirit.

BREADS & SPREADS

SPICY PEPPER JELLY

½	cup finely chopped hot peppers	6	cups sugar
¾	cup finely chopped bell peppers	1	pkg. (6 oz.) fruit pectin
1 ¼	cups cider vinegar	•	Several drops red food coloring

Pour vinegar and sugar into a large saucepan; add peppers. Boil for 2 to 3 minutes. Skim off excess foam. Stir in the fruit pectin and cook 2 more minutes. Add food coloring, and pour into hot jars. Seal and place on a rack in a canner, filled with simmering water. Cover jars with 2″ hot water. Cover canner and bring to a boil; simmer 5 minutes. Remove and cool. Excellent with crackers and cream cheese.

ANADAMA BREAD

(A Pennsylvania Tradition)

2	pkgs. dry yeast		2	tsp. salt
1	Tbsp. sugar		1	cup cornmeal
1 ½	cups warm water, not too hot		2	cups graham flour
4	Tbsp. butter		2	cups all-purpose flour, or more
½	cup molasses			

Dissolve yeast and sugar in 1/2 cup warm water and let stand for 5 minutes. Add butter, molasses, and salt to remaining warm water in a large bowl. Stir in yeast mixture and cornmeal. Gradually add the flour and mix well. It will seem difficult, but beat this sticky mixture vigorously. Turn out onto a floured board. Fold the dough over, again and again, scraping under the dough until it can be kneaded. Knead until the dough is easy and springy to handle. Shape into a ball, place it into a buttered bowl and turning it to grease, it on all sides. Cover with a clean towel and let rise in a warm corner of the kitchen for 1½ hours or until double in size. Punch down and turn out on a floured board. Knead for 2 minutes, and divide in half. Shape each half into loaf pans. Cover and let rise until double in bulk. Bake at 400 degrees for 10 minutes, reduce heat to 350 degrees, and bake for 40 minutes. The loaves should sound hollow when tapped. Place on cooling racks.

PEAR BUTTER

½	gallon pears, peeled & quartered		2	gallons water
2 ½	lbs. sugar		•	Cloves, cinnamon, nutmeg

Combine pears, sugar, and water in a large saucepan. Bring mixture to a boil, and cook over low heat until it thickens. If desired, add cloves, cinnamon, and nutmeg. Pour into hot quart jars and seal. Place jars on a rack in a canner filled with simmering water; cover with 2" hot water. Cover and bring the water back to a boil. Simmer gently for 5 minutes. Cool jars on a towel for 12 to 24 hours undisturbed.

RELISHES & PICKLES

ZUCCHINI RELISH

10	cups zucchini, grated	2 ½	cups vinegar
4	large onions, chopped	2	Tbsp. celery seed
4	red and green peppers, diced	2	Tbsp. dry mustard
5	Tbsp. salt	1	tsp. turmeric
•	Water	2	Tbsp. fruit pectin
4 ½	cups sugar		

Place zucchini, vegetables, and salt in a large saucepan. Cover with water, bring to a boil, let cool and drain. Add sugar and remaining ingredients, except fruit pectin. Cook for 30 minutes. Mix in fruit pectin. Put in hot jars, and seal. Place jars on canner rack in boiling water with 2" hot water to cover jars. Cover canner loosely, and bring water to a boil. Boil for 20 minutes. Cool jars on a towel for 12 to 24 hours.

PICKLED CANTALOUPE

3	large cantaloupes, peeled & cubed	6	cups sugar
4	cups water	1	tsp. salt
1	cup vinegar		

Heat water, vinegar, sugar, and salt until dissolved. Pack cantaloupe into hot jars and add syrup. Place sealed jars on rack, in a canner, in hot water. Cover jars with 2" hot water. Cover canner loosely and bring water to a boil. Boil for 20 minutes. Cool jars on a towel for 12 to 24 hours.

CHOW CHOW

1	cup navy beans	2	cups pearl onions
2	cups dried kidney beans	2	cups cabbage, chopped
2	cups string beans	2	cups sweet gherkins, chopped
1	cup yellow wax beans	5	cups sugar
2	cups cauliflower, chopped	2 ½	cups cider vinegar
2	cups celery, chopped	1 ½	cups water
2	cups red and green peppers, chopped	2	Tbsp. mustard seed
2	cups carrots, sliced	1	Tbsp. celery seed
2	cups fresh corn kernels	1	tsp. turmeric

Cook all vegetables separately, until tender and drain. Combine sugar and remaining ingredients in a kettle; bring mixture to a boil and pour over vegetables. Pack vegetables into hot jars; seal and place jars on a rack in a canner, in hot, but not boiling water. Cover with 2" hot water. Place lid loosely on canner and bring to a boil; boil gently for 10 to 15 minutes. Remove jars from canner and let sit undisturbed for 12 to 24 hours.

"Often those who speak least on earth are best known in heaven."

SUMMER STRAWBERRY JAM

2	cups strawberries, crushed	¾	cup water
4	cups sugar	⅓	cup fruit pectin

Stir sugar into fruit. Set aside for 10 minutes, stirring occasionally. Mix water and fruit pectin in a small saucepan. Bring mixture to a boil, and stir for 1 minute. Stir hot fruit pectin mixture into the fruit mixture. Stir constantly for 3 minutes. Fill all containers to within ½ inch of the top. Wipe off top edges of containers; quickly cover with lids. Let stand at room temperature for 24 hours, then place in the freezer. After opening, store in the refrigerator.

MUSTARD PICKLES

10	medium cucumbers	2	Tbsp. mustard seed
•	Water	1	Tbsp. mixed whole
•	Salt		all spice
4	cups vinegar	2	cups sugar

Peel cucumbers, remove seeds and cut cucumbers into long strips. Cover strips with water in a bowl and sprinkle liberally with salt. Allow them to stand overnight; drain. Combine vinegar and remaining ingredients in a large sauce pan, bring to a boil and remove from heat. Add cucumber strips and pack into hot jars. Place sealed jars on a canner rack in boiling water, covered by 2" hot water. Cover canner loosely; bring water to a boil and boil for 20 minutes. Cool jars on a towel for 12 to 24 hours.

AMISH CHILDREN

The Amish people believe that God has called them to a life of faith, dedication, humility and service. It is the belief in God's personal interest in their lives and communities which hold them together, in spite of the many forces that could pull them apart.

Children are deeply cherished among the Amish. Most families are large, averaging seven children. Children are viewed as "a gift from the Lord." Many babies are born at home, but hospitals are permitted and are used more frequently today.

An Amish baby is not baptized because the Amish practice adult believers baptism. Relatives and friends flock to visit the new baby. Small presents may be shared, often food or clothing. Biblical names are traditionally favored.

At first glance, Amish children may appear to lead restricted lives cut off from the opportunities to fulfill their individual destinies. However, few children in our world today lead as contented and fulfilled lives as most Amish children do, surrounded by security, clear expectations, numerous role models both inside and outside their immediate families, and a sense of hope and belonging. Amish youth, like teenagers everywhere, pass through a time of identity search. Amish young people many times face a great deal of tension as they decide whether to stay in the Amish world that has nurtured them or join the "English."

In their late teens, some Amish youth may join a "crowd," sometimes numbering as many as one hundred or more. Most crowds conform to traditional Amish ways. These youth attend Sunday evening singing and engage in traditional recreation such as softball, volleyball, hiking and skating.

Many children in the larger American society grow up being challenged, "to get someplace in life," to be somebody. These ideas are alien to Amish society. Many modern ideas and habits signal pride in Amish eyes. Jewelry, wristwatches, fashionable clothing, and personal photographs accentuate individuality and call attention to one's self. To "be somebody" is to become a humble, responsible, loving member of the Amish community.

SWEET RETREAT

LEMON MERINGUE PIE

3	Tbsp. cornstarch	1¼	cups water
1½	cups sugar	6	Tbsp. sugar
1	lemon	1	9-inch pie crust,
3	eggs, separated		baked

Squeeze juice from lemon and grate rind. Boil rind in water. Mix cornstarch and sugar. Separate the eggs and beat yolks, then add to the cornstarch mixture. Remove lemon rind from water. Add water to cornstarch mixture and cook in double boiler. Fill pie crust. Beat egg whites until stiff, add sugar. Spread over the pie and brown. Bake at 425 degrees for 30 to 40 minutes, or until done.

RHUBARB PIE

2	cups chopped rhubarb	1	cup walnuts
1	cup sugar	⅓	cup brown sugar
1	egg, slightly beaten	3	Tbsp. honey
1	Tbsp. flour	3	Tbsp. butter
½	tsp. salt	3	Tbsp. whipping cream
1	tsp. lemon juice	1	9-inch pie crust

Mix together sugar, flour, and egg. Add rhubarb and lemon juice. Pour into the pie shell and bake at 425 degrees for 20 minutes. Mix the remaining ingredients, except the walnuts, and boil until it thickens. Add walnuts and spread this mixture over the pie and bake at 350 degrees for 20 minutes or until brown.

WALNUT SPONGE CAKE

6	eggs, separated	½	tsp. salt
½	cup cold water	¾	cup walnuts,
1 ½	cups sugar		chopped fine
½	tsp. vanilla	¾	tsp. cream of tartar
1 ¼	cups flour, sifted		

Beat egg yolks until thick and lemon colored. Add water and sugar and beat well; gradually add vanilla. Fold in flour, salt, and nuts. Beat egg whites and cream of tartar until stiff; then fold into yolk mixture. Pour into a greased pan and bake at 325 degrees for 1 hour.

"If you see a friend without a smile, please give him one of yours."

MOLASSES MELT COOKIES

5	cups flour	¼	cup hot water
1	Tbsp. nutmeg	1	cup molasses
1	Tbsp. cinnamon	¾	cup sugar
2	Tbsp. baking soda	¾	cup shortening

Sift together flour, nutmeg, and cinnamon. Dissolve soda in hot water, and stir into the flour mixture. In a separate bowl, combine molasses, sugar, and shortening, then add to the flour mixture, stirring well. Drop by teaspoonfuls onto a greased baking sheet. Bake at 375 degrees for 8 to 10 minutes or until brown.

CARAMEL TAFFY CANDY

1	cup brown sugar	1	Tbsp. vanilla
¾	cup white corn syrup	•	Nuts, chopped
1 ½	cups cream	1	pkg. chocolate chips,
2	Tbsp. butter		melted

Bring brown sugar, white corn syrup and ½ cup cream to a rolling boil. Add ½ cup cream and boil to 234 degrees; add remaining cream and boil to 234 degrees (soft ball stage). Remove from heat; add butter and vanilla. Add nuts of your choice and pour into a greased 9-inch square pan. Cool and cut in squares. Dip squares into the melted chocolate. Sprinkle chopped nuts on each square and place on wax paper to dry.

"Sons are a heritage from the Lord, children a reward from him."

-Psalms 127:3

FUDGE BROWN SUGAR CANDY

1	cup brown sugar	¼	tsp. maple flavoring
1	cup sugar	1	tsp. vanilla
¾	cup milk	¾	cup pecans or nut
•	Pinch of salt		of your choice
2	Tbsp. butter		

Combine the first 4 ingredients in a sauce pan and bring to a boil, 234 degrees (soft ball stage). Remove from heat and add butter, maple flavoring, and vanilla. Mix well and let cool to lukewarm. Stir in pecans, walnuts or nuts of your choice.

JUMPING JUMBLES

4	eggs, beaten	1	tsp. baking soda
1	lb. sugar	½	tsp. salt
¾	cup butter, softened	1	tsp. lemon extract
6	cups flour		

Cream eggs, sugar, and butter together. Sift together flour, baking soda, and salt; add to sugar mixture; mix well. Blend in lemon extract. Roll the dough out thin on a floured surface. Use cookie cutters to cut into desired shapes. Bake at 375 degrees for 6 minutes.